Water Wise

EARTH'S OCEANS

Gail Parman

PowerKiDS press

Published in 2027 by
The Rosen Publishing Group, Inc.
2544 Clinton Street, Buffalo, NY 14224

Designer: Beeline Media and Design
Editor: Tricia Hoffman

Portions of this work were originally authored by Peter Castellano and published as *Where's the Water?: Earth's Oceans*. All new material in this edition is authored by Gail Parman.

Photo credits: Cover, p. 1 Andrey Yurlov/Shutterstock.com; Cover, p. 1 SaltyArts Design/Shutterstock.com; cover, p. 1, 4, 6, 8, 10, 12, 14, 16, 18, 20, 21, 24 (wave) vectorstuff/Shutterstock.com; p. 5 Viacheslav Lopatin/Shutterstock.com; p. 5 buradaki/Shutterstock.com; p. 7 Vibe Images/Shutterstock.com; p. 9 Ethan Daniels/Shutterstock.com; p. 9 Yarr65/Shutterstock.com; p. 11 Vladimir Potapeknko/Shutterstock.com; p. 11 zelvan/Shutterstock.com; p. 13 Sven Hansche/Shutterstock.com; p. 15 Allen.G/Shutterstock.com; p. 16 Designua/Shutterstock.com; p. 17 maks_ph/Shutterstock.com; p. 19 Urbano Creativo/Shutterstock.com; p. 21 Photoongraphy/Shutterstock.com

Cataloging-in-Publication Data
Names: Parman, Gail.
Title: Earth's oceans / Gail Parman.
Description: Buffalo, New York : PowerKids Press, 2027. | Series: Water wise | Includes glossary and index.
Identifiers: ISBN 9781499458282 (pbk.) | ISBN 9781499458299 (library bound) | ISBN 9781499458305 (ebook)
Subjects: LCSH: Ocean--Juvenile literature.
Classification: LCC GC21.5 P377 2027 | DDC 551.46--dc23

Printed in China

CPSIA Compliance Information: Batch #QSPK27. For Further Information contact Rosen Publishing at 1-800-237-9932.

Contents

The Global Ocean

Today, there are five named oceans: the Pacific, the Atlantic, the Indian, the Southern, and the Arctic. But if you looked at Earth from space, you'd see just one body of water that is entirely connected. This is often called the global ocean.

Geologists, map makers, and world leaders have set boundaries to separate this large body of water into five different oceans. This makes it easier to talk about where things are on Earth.

Go with the Flow

The total length of the world's coastlines is about 315,000 miles (507,000 km). That is big enough to circle the equator 12 times!

A giant body of salt water covers more than 70 percent of Earth. It looks much more like a blue planet than a green one!

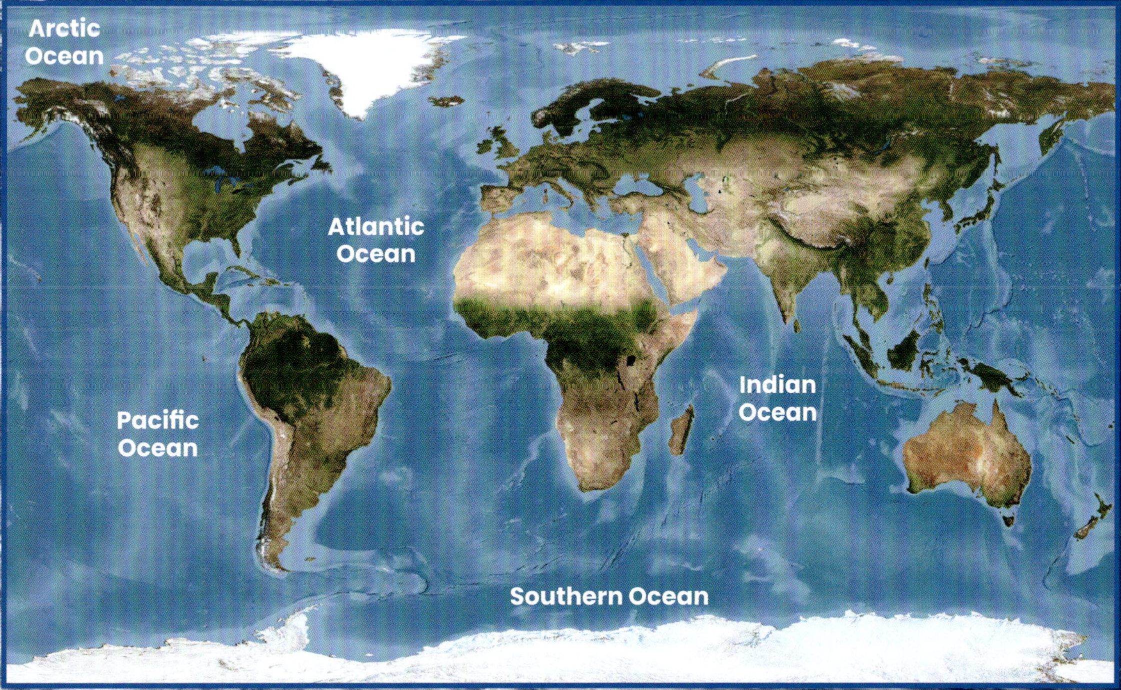

Basins, Trenches, and Ridges

Think of the bottom of the ocean as a large bowl. The oceans' water is held in very large basins, or dips, in Earth's surface. These basins are shaped like circular or oval-shaped bowls. Any water in the basin does not escape it.

Basins have changed a lot over time as the large plates that make up Earth's **crust** have moved. The movement of these plates has created deep **trenches**.

As plates smash into one another, they form ridges. Ridges look like huge underwater mountain chains. Underwater ridges sometimes reach the ocean's surface as islands.

Go with the Flow

The Mid-Atlantic Ridge formed where the two plates that make up the floor of the Atlantic Ocean meet. It's about 10,000 miles (16,100 km) long!

The Hawaiian islands are home to some of the tallest mountains in the world.

The Deep Pacific

The Pacific Ocean is the largest named ocean. It covers more of Earth than all the land put together. It touches four **continents**: Asia, Australia, North America, and South America. It is also the deepest ocean, and is home to the deepest spot on Earth.

The Pacific Ocean **stretches** from the Arctic areas in the north to the Antarctic areas in the south. Its waters cover a lot of **climates** and **temperatures**, from the warm tropical waters near the equator to the frigid polar regions.

The ocean's basin is surrounded by the Ring of Fire, which includes 75 percent of Earth's **volcanoes**! The volcanic activity causes tsunamis, which are huge waves that can destroy anything in their path if they hit land.

Go with the Flow

Pacific comes from a Latin word meaning "peaceful."

Iliape is an active volcano on an island in Indonesia.
It is part of the Ring of Fire.

The Awesome Atlantic

The Atlantic Ocean covers about 20 percent of Earth's surface. It is the world's second largest ocean. It is settled between North and South America in the west, and Europe and Africa in the east.

The line of **latitude** that divides Earth, the equator, is used to separate the Atlantic Ocean into the North Atlantic and South Atlantic. A massive underwater mountain range called the Mid-Atlantic Ridge runs through the Atlantic from north to south. It extends from the Arctic Ocean in the north to the Southern Ocean in the south.

Go with the Flow

The Atlantic is the saltiest of all the oceans.

The Atlantic Ocean formed about 180 million years ago. It is home to some of the biggest islands on Earth, including Greenland, Great Britain, and Newfoundland.

The Warm Indian Ocean

The Indian Ocean is the third-largest ocean on Earth. About one-fifth of the water covering Earth is part of the Indian Ocean. It's bordered by Asia to the north, Africa to the west, and Australia to the east.

The Indian Ocean borders three of the four other oceans. It touches the Atlantic Ocean around the southern tip of Africa. It meets the Pacific Ocean to the east of Australia and Asia. It touches the Southern Ocean north of Antarctica.

Go with the Flow

Of the world's three largest oceans, the Indian Ocean is considered the youngest.

Because of its location along the equator, the Indian Ocean is the warmest.

The "New" Southern

About 25 years ago, scientists decided to give the ocean waters surrounding Antarctica its own name. The Southern Ocean, sometimes known as the Antarctic Ocean, became the world's fifth named ocean. Its waters connect the Pacific, Atlantic, and Indian Oceans.

The Southern Ocean's northernmost **boundary** was set at 60°S latitude, making it the fourth-largest ocean on Earth. It is about twice as large as the United States!

Go with the Flow

The Southern Ocean's temperature is commonly between 28 and 50 degrees Fahrenheit (–2 and 10 degrees Celsius). You wouldn't want to swim in that!!

Antarctica and the Southern Ocean are home to many animals that thrive in cold temperatures, such as these Adelie penguins.

The Chilly Arctic

The Arctic Ocean is the coldest ocean on Earth. It's almost always covered with ice that can be nearly 10 feet (3 m) thick!

The Arctic Ocean is the smallest and shallowest ocean on Earth. It's only about one-sixth the size of the Indian Ocean. The deepest point that's been recorded is only about 18,050 feet (5,500 m) deep.

Go with the Flow

The Arctic Ocean is almost completely surrounded by land, including North America, Greenland, Europe, and Asia.

This icebreaker vessel is a special ship that can break through ice-covered waters. Other ships can get stuck in the deep ice of the Arctic.

The Smaller Seas

What's the difference between an ocean and a sea? Seas are smaller than oceans. They are most often places where the ocean meets land or where land encloses ocean water. There are inland seas too, such as the Caspian Sea. All seas contain salt water, even those that are inland.

Two of the biggest seas on Earth are the Mediterranean and the Caribbean. The Mediterranean Sea is found between Europe, northern Africa, and southwestern Asia. It connects to the Atlantic Ocean between Spain and Morocco. The Caribbean Sea has Central America to its west and South America to its south. It is found near the equator where it's hot.

Go with the Flow
About 97 percent of all the water on Earth is found in ocean water and sea ice.

The warm waters of the Caribbean Sea are commonly around 80 degrees Fahrenheit (27 degrees Celsius).

Ocean Health

It is estimated that about 80 percent of the world's population lives within 60 miles (96.6 km) of an ocean's coast. Humans have a huge impact on the health of the oceans.

Pollution, such as the burning of **fossil fuels**, has caused Earth to grow warmer. Over time, rising temperatures cause the ice to melt, increasing ocean levels. This harms the animals and plants that live in the oceans, as well as the people and land around them.

Groups around the world help clean up pollution along coastlines and work to reduce fossil fuel use. Everyone can help keep the world's oceans healthy.

Go with the Flow

Scientists have found that the amount of ice covering the Arctic Ocean shrinks about 8 percent every 10 years.

The Five Oceans

	Percentage of the Global Ocean	Average Depth
Pacific	46.6 percent	2.5 miles (4 km)
Atlantic	23.5 percent	2.2 miles (3.6 km)
Indian	19.5 percent	2.3 miles (3.7 km)
Southern	6.1 percent	2 miles (3.2 km)
Arctic	4.3 percent	0.75 mile (1.2 km)

Glossary

boundary: a place that marks the limit of something

climate: the average weather conditions of a place over a period of time

continent: one of Earth's seven great landmasses

crust: the outer shell of a planet

fossil fuel: matter formed over millions of years from plant and animal remains that is burned for power

geologist: someone who studies geology, or the science that studies the history of Earth and its life as recorded in rocks

latitude: the imaginary lines that run east and west above and below the equator

stretch: to reach across

temperature: how hot or cold something is

trench: a long, narrow cut in the ground

volcano: an opening in a planet's surface through which hot, liquid rock sometimes flows

Fact Check

1. All of the ocean water on Earth is often called the____________.
   a. global ocean
   b. big ocean
   c. connected ocean

2. Which ocean is the youngest?
   a. Pacific
   b. Indian
   c. Arctic

3. Which ocean is almost completely surrounded by land?
   a. Arctic
   b. Atlantic
   c. Southern

Answers: 1. a, 2. b, 3. a

On the Internet

Ocean Facts
www.natgeokids.com/uk/discover/geography/general-geography/ocean-facts/
Dive into the top 10 ocean facts with National Geographic Kids.

Oceans for Kids
ducksters.com/geography/oceans.php
Read more about Earth's oceans here.

Index